Embody

SONEE SINGH

First published in Australia in 2021
by MMH Press
Waikiki, WA 6169

www.mmhpress.com

Cover design by: Jennifer Dinsdale
Interior design by: Ida Jensson

A catalogue record for this work is available from the National Library of Australia

National Library of Australia Catalogue-in-Publication data:
Embody/Sonee Singh

978-0-6451484-9-7 (Hardback)
978-0-6451484-3-5 (Paperback)
978-0-6451484-4-2 (Ebook)

Embody

SONEE SINGH

First published in Australia in 2021
by MMH Press
Waikiki, WA 6169

www.mmhpress.com

Cover design by: Jennifer Dinsdale
Interior design by: Ida Jensson

A catalogue record for this work is available from the National Library of Australia

National Library of Australia Catalogue-in-Publication data:
Embody/Sonee Singh

978-0-6451484-9-7 (Hardback)
978-0-6451484-3-5 (Paperback)
978-0-6451484-4-2 (Ebook)

For My Parents

Who are

There

Always

Without whom

I wouldn't be

Who I am

They are

My Heart

Something unexpected awoke in me when Covid-19 surged upon us. I was alone for four months of the pandemic. Many days, the only person I faced was myself. It seemed like I had no choice but to look upon every aspect of who I was. I was met with a compelling urge to write about it. The shape it took was poetry–something I never thought I would be able to write.

Yet I did, exploring all aspects of how to embody what I was experiencing. The highs and lows. The joys and sorrows. The hope and despair. It brought about a transformation. It felt like I was changing but perhaps it brought out a side of me I didn't know I had; a part of me that had remained hidden, waiting patiently for me to prompt it.

In the moment, I was unaware. I merely followed the heartstrings of my soul, listened to the inner calling of my being. Only afterwards did I realize the poems were healing and that healing had a shape, releasing from me what I needed to let go of and bringing into me what I needed to move forward.

These poems are organized according to the seven chakras–energetic centers in our body plane.

Chakras

Energetic wheels of life

Vortex spiraling through the eye of our being

A seed delivered into human experience

Our purpose to grow and expand

Roots seeping deep into the soil

Canopy reaching high into the sky

Kundalini life-force surging in between

First, Muladhara, root

Anchor, ground, secure, safe, stable, support, physical

Second, Svadhisthana, sacral

Create, procreate, relate, emote, trust, flow, manifest

Third, Manipura, solar plexus

Focus, willpower, drive, intention, confidence, life-force, inner light

Fourth, Anahata, heart

Give love, receive love, self-love, connect, compassion, service, altruism

Fifth, Vishuddha, throat

Communicate, express, voice, creativity, truth, openness, purity

Sixth, Ajna, third eye

Intuition, knowing, inner guidance, perception,
imagination, sight, inspiration

Seventh, Sahasrara, crown

Spiritual connection, higher consciousness, wisdom,
divine, faith, presence, bliss

First, Muladhara, root

Anchor, ground, secure, safe, stable, support, physical

Security

Adrift in the wind
Left to chance
Without a net

A matter of the mind
It too shifts
Draws from the void

A moving sense of control
Morphs with circumstances
Ever evolving perception

A grasp in the darkness
From the unknown
Security comes

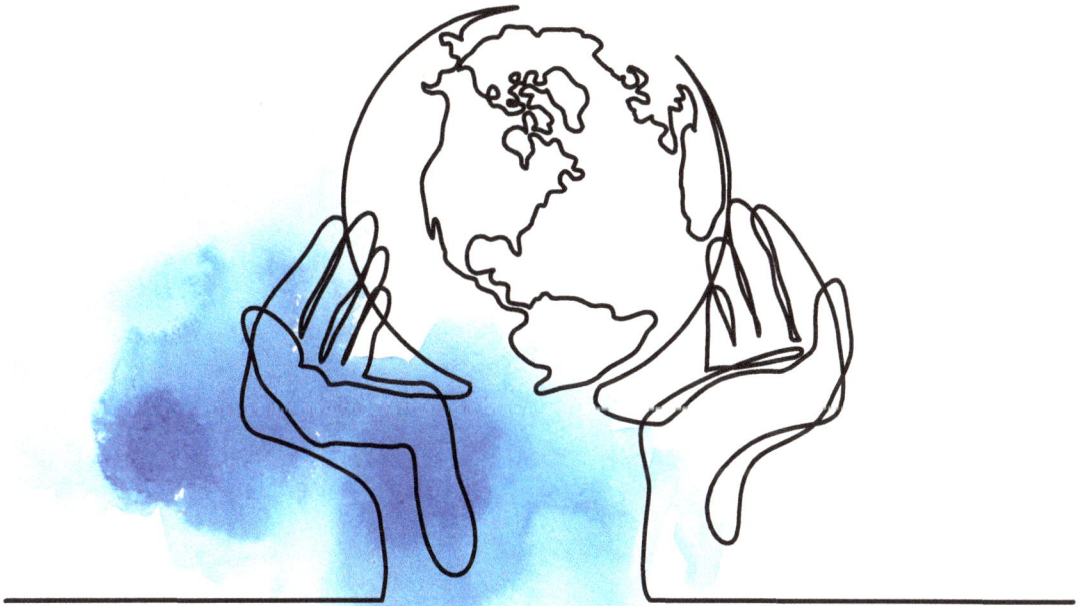

All is well

All is well

I am meant to feel

Despite the numbers

Rising fear and anger

Inequity and injustice

Shake the world

A hurricane tornado typhoon

Clearing the space

For kindness

Inclusivity and harmony

It's what we need

An accepting community

A compassionate must

To get everything back

All is well

So much

So much
In my life
Grateful for

Deep and restful
8-hour sleep
Not waking once

Steaming spicy chai
Warms my soul
Dipped in biscuits

Smell of butter
Air popped corn
Side of romantic comedy

A phone call
At the exact time
I was thinking of them

Unsure when packing
What to keep
What to donate

Stacking up piles
Books to keep
Haven't yet read

Meal plans spurred
What's in the fridge
Laden to the handle

Knowing no matter
What happens
I'm provided for

Abundance

Able to live
Having all
That is needed

Joy and love
Provide resources
Fuel our potential

Friends and family
Constant and regular
Show love and support

Plenty at the table
To nourish and please
Feeding the heart

A body that moves

Guiding our lives

Health is abundance

Certain things are forgotten

Yet they never run out

Always can and always have

Possibilities are limitless

Choices endless

Make us full

Overflowing

The universe

Always provides

Thank you

For my small moments
And big ones too
The aroma of coffee
Waking to a new day

For keeping me safe
And close to my loved ones
Through tumultuous times
Remaining supportive

For unburdening me
Forgiving my sins and others
Because the pain of one
Is the pain of all

For teaching me discernment
Building healthy boundaries
A compassionate embrace
Kindly connecting us all

For all of my dreams
Those that come true
And those that tantalize
Entertaining day and night

For making my life
All that has happened
Brought to this place
To be who I am

Watermelon tourmaline

Like a watermelon tourmaline

Constantly connected

Plugged-in to source

In a grounded way

While opening hearts

The beauty of a watermelon

Green on the edges

Fuchsia on the inside

Balancing out

Masculine and feminine

Watermelon tourmaline speaks

To everyone and everything

Healing with compassion

Peaceful and calm

In the moment

Sunrise and sunset

Dawning of the day
Settling into night

Colors are mystic
Magic is possible

Miracles and grace
Are instant

Tea

Feeds my soul
Like water to a plant
Helping me grow
Up towards the sun
Deepening my roots
Down into the earth

Tired

Tired

Feeling

   Unseen

   Unloved

   Lonely

   Irrelevant

   Forsaken

   Forgotten

Time

Controls

   Unravel

   Unaccepted

   Cannot

   Self-less

   Criticized

   Helpless

Please

Surrender

   Untether

   Unabashed

   Accept

   Discern

   Guide

   Reunite

Body

Transforms as we evolve

A transient home

Nourishment and more

This time on earth

From a pea in a pod

Until ashes and bones

Ailing to redirect

Encouraging strength

Tossing and tumbling

Growth is life

Purposeful

Whole and complete

Taking us places

Caring for us

Coming and going

Being our seat

Always imparting

Love and graces

Yoga

My body wakens
Moves with no grace

I push to flatten
And stretch with the earth

Muscles tense and release
I struggle with ease

Feeding my being

My body strains
In every new stance

I drain what accumulates
Through every count

Work through the cycles
I quiver with ease

Feeding my spirit

My body expresses
In a moving machine

I breathe in and out
Exerting my will

Leaning and reaching
I am at ease

Feeding my soul

Gaia

We are part of it
It is part of us

Essentially so
So vital

Gives life with ease
Eases breath to treasure

We've grown apart
A part we weren't meant to

A separation we created

Creation roots we ignored

We must push to embrace

Embrace what made us

Paying tribute to it

It is all there is

A given day

Moments tumble
Through emotions
In a given day
I embody them all

I wake up fierce
Ready to conquer
Vanquish the dark
Riding my tiger

I steep with my brews
Nurturing my being
Action expands into
Becoming myself

My eyes teeter to close
Tiger astride
In the spirit of knowing
I surrender it all

An afternoon

It is so humid

Even paper grows weak

Under the watch

Of the Washington Square heat

My breath struggles

Ignored by an itch

As if a critter

Plunged into my skin

The air is too dense

Even for pincers

To engage in any kind

Of moving assault

Sweat trickles my scalp
And makes its way down
A sticky mess settling
At the edge of my shirt

It seems like a lifetime
Since St. Phillips sang
For the noon hour feast
Prodding me here

A breeze rolls in
Temporarily cooling
Hoping I make it
To the 1pm toll

I stumble over cobble
A reminder of what stood
For hundreds of years
Through this same heat

Second, Svadhisthana, sacral

Create, procreate, relate, emote, trust, flow, manifest

How I feel

I have them

Feelings

Yet I have forgotten

The feels still feel

And when they do

And I refuse to see

They burrow within

Rearing in other forms

Head pounding

Teeth grinding

Soreness when I stretch my arms

Digging into my hips in yogi squat

They have to find a way

Seeking attention

Gently at first

Tap tap tapping

That I ignore

The clamor grows

In an unsuspecting puppy dog pose

That tears through my triceps

33 seconds is all it takes

A sob breaks

Cracking avoidance, neglect, numbness

Awkward at first

Blinded by the light

In the dark for too long

But no longer

Not anymore

And the tears stream

One after another

My body collapses

Chest heaving over my knees

It's been a while

When the tears stop

I feel lighter

I've made space

A smile creeps

Slowly taking over

I've made it through

Until the next wave

I'm still

Once again

I've found peace

Overwhelm

Internet says no connection

When WiFi has all bars

Just as I was wondering what is possible

The fridge spills out water

Defrost from a solitary spark plug

Just as I was feeling out of control

The light turns off fully and flickers back on

When I'm nowhere near the switch

Just as I wondered if I'm forsaken

A shiver spreads like thunder

Visible sparks in the dark

Just as I cut off the last threads of sleep

Spirit is made of energy

Same as electricity and love

Just to remind I can do this and more

Cheerful

Positive and cheerful without a pill

Otherwise I would be ill

My cheeriness comes with a chill

Like a view after climbing a hill

Better to be peaceful than ill

I am peaceful and chill

Like a breeze atop a hill

Otherwise I would be ill

Grief

Death is not necessary

For grief

It fills me

So much it spills

I see your sadness

They say

As if I lost someone

I didn't

At least not in this life

I have

Lost many

But it's not why I grieve

Yet it fills me

I ache for myself

Burn to ashes

Churn in the fire

To be dissolved forever

Forgotten

Alone

Hoping one day

Someone will notice

Someone will remember

That I'm here

That one day

Maybe

I will rise again

Hope

Sleepless organizing
Ceaseless review of plans

Rooms reduced to boxes
Cold meals over bubble wrap

Muscles ache in exhaustion
Adrenaline moves the spirit

Parting with routines
Bittersweet excitement

Hope filled beginnings
Maybe this time will be it

Calm

I am calm
Contemplate my plan
To not have one

To embrace life
Moment by moment
Can't handle more

I look further out
Can't help my mind
Filled with doubt

Breaking the calm
I want in my heart
In my mind

It often runs away

From me

Then I am awash

With worry

Fear

And anxiety

Of what is to come

How

And when

I can't quite see

Muddy and uncertain

Far out of reach

Then comes the typhoon

Flooding my nights

Thundering through my sleep

My eyes peel open

Having no reprieve

Burning and arid

I am not deserted

How can it be

I see it all around me

My goosebumps high

Feeling within

Love surrounding me

Divine entourage

Forever in place

Constant and faithful

Meet them at their gaze

See myself reflected back

And all there is

Dispel the unease

Usher in the peace

And assurance

That I am safe

Guided

And protected

The darkness turns

A snug hammock

Love and security

I lift myself

Arms open wide

Surrendering

To the quiet

Stillness

And calm

Skies

Dense and dark
Popped by lightning
Heavens thunder upon us
Casting away shadows

So dark it feels like night
Sun pushed away
Lights turn out
Embracing the dark

A solitary moment of tremble
How long will it last
This and the other thunder
Lit up with the crash

What I hear

You

    Are ugly

    Are hairy

    Are so eager to please

    Are fat

    Have no personality

    Should be more like her

    Should be perfect

    Shouldn't ask questions

    Speak differently

    Carry yourself differently

    Don't know how to dress

    Only worry about yourself

    Can't settle

    Will always be alone

    Are better off alone

    Are always on the go

You touch people

Your

Your food is strange

Your lunch smells

Your accent is weird

Your life is unique

But your face is pretty

Confusion

Where are you from?

Where do you live?

Do you go to church or temple?

Do you eat beef?

Do you only eat vegetables?

Are you a good Indian girl?

Are you loose or a prude?

Do you have a backbone?

Why aren't you married yet?

What happened to you?

There is something special about you

Phone Call

I love our calls

Because we always find

A reason to laugh

No matter how bleak

The talks we have

Lane to friends

Cross a stitch

Cross the lane

Lane to lead

Lane to the stars

Stars above

Stars so bright

Bright for my eyes

Bright in the sky

Sky in which I used to fly

Sky so clear tonight

Tonight I stare

Tonight I look out my window

Window to the world

Window that tells of the outside

Outside seems so far

Outside is so warm

Warm that I miss

Warm like my hugs

Hugs that I love to give

Hugs I too miss

Miss so much

Miss my life

Life was lovely

Life was vivid

Vivid with people

Vivid with memories

Memories of people

Memories of special places

Places near me

Places far away

Away from where I am

Away from myself

Myself with others

Myself with my thoughts

Thoughts of what I could learn

Thoughts of new beginnings

Beginning again

Beginning in a new city

City with possibilities

City offering new dreams

Dreams of what can be

Dreams of what is possible

Possible to transform

Possible to start a new

A new way of life

A new set of friends

Friends to keep me company

Friends to entertain

Entertain

Company

Travel

I am able to travel
Everywhere
Not in body
Because of rona

In mind and spirit
I journey
Through the past
Other lives

Memories and recollections
Reminders of who I was
Where I lived
Who I was with

I create a vision

Of what will come

What I wish to create

My musings

I come back now

Feeling at home

Knowing I am

Where I am meant to be

Magic

Magic

Leads to clarity

Something from nothing

Where there was not

There now is

Trust

When we don't believe

Lost hope and feel lost

To keep us going

Having faith

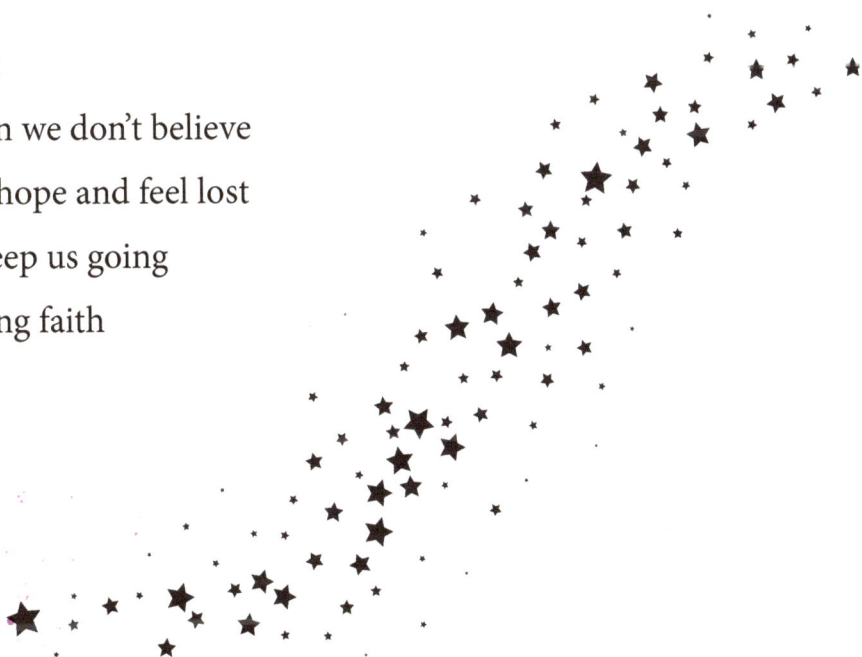

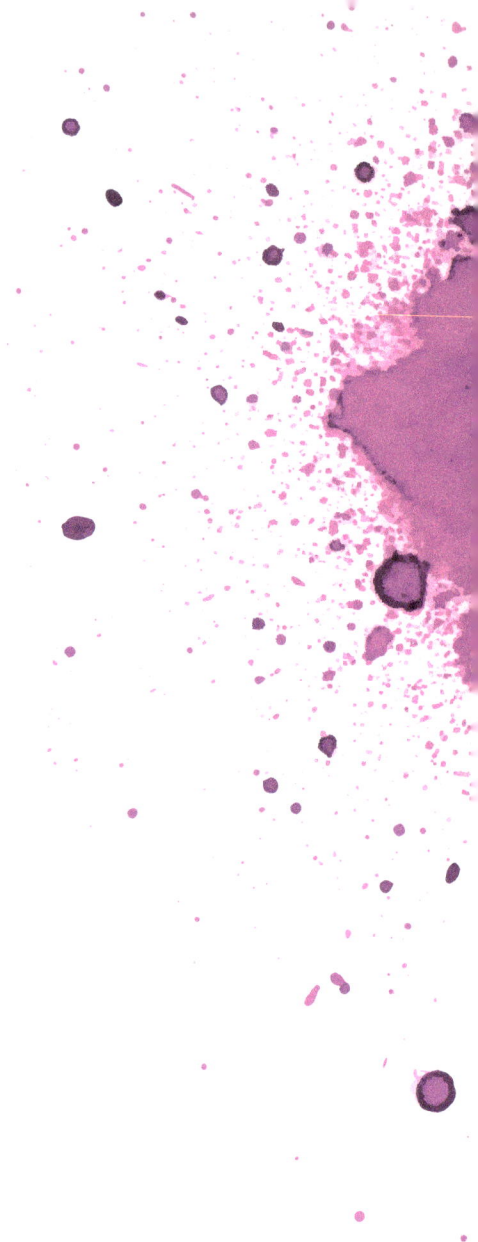

Surprise
Seemingly out of no where
Yet direct from Grace
When we most need
A light shines

Bumps
Sends shivers of awareness
A confirmation
We are cared for
Not alone

Miracles
Dreams come true
But bigger and better
Than imagined
Trust in magic

Third, Manipura, solar plexus

Focus, willpower, drive, intention, confidence, life-force, inner light

Empower

I thought power
Was rather mean
Sorry I was

Thought to misuse
It's rather not
Energy it is

Empower means to
Bring to me
Energy for good

A face

I have one of those faces
That expresses many places

Universal in its reach
Because brown is wide in reach

There are so many of us
In a range of shades and tones

All browns are not the same
So many traces and places

People of color
Even white is a color

Language, culture, and food
Brown but not the same

Options

Do what feels good
Even if it irritates

Be mindful
It's their choice to unfollow

The aim is not
To be liked by all

All you can do
Care for intention

All you must do
You choose you

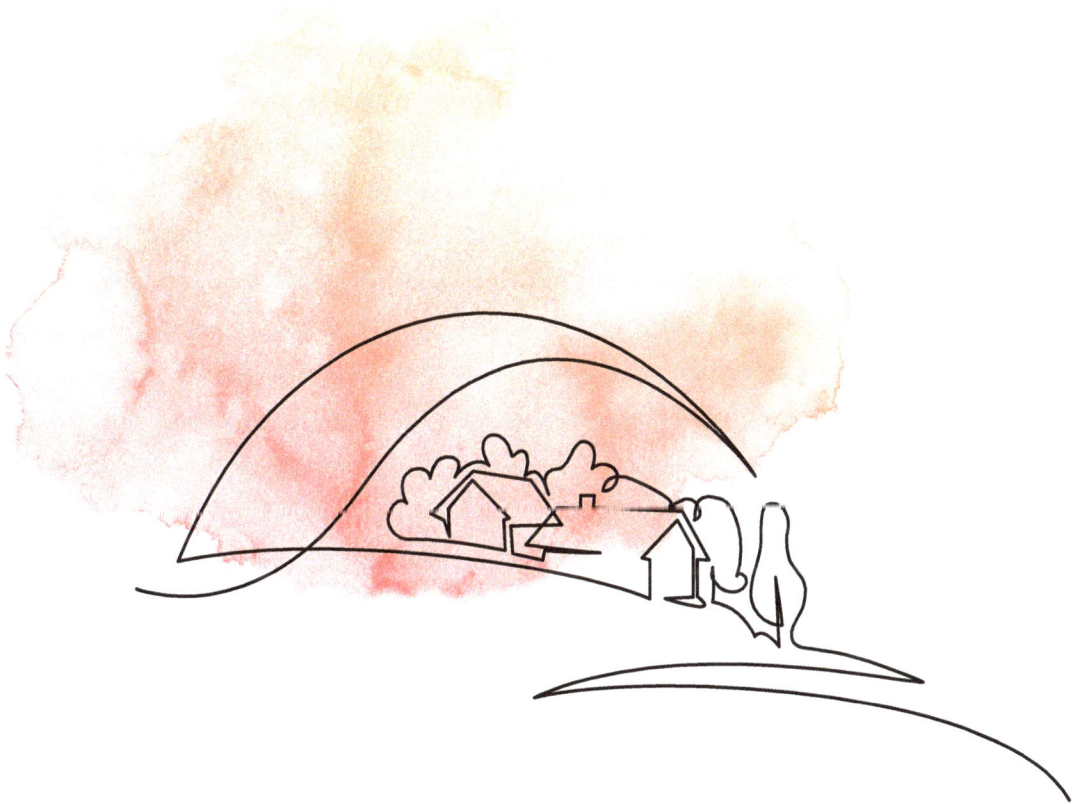

My place

When I was younger I didn't know

Where my place was in the world

The larger puzzle board was lost

To the little piece that was me

I couldn't see where I fit

Where are you from they'd want to know

I couldn't name just one place in the world

That I felt could host

All that was in me

I threw it all into a pit

To see which place would grow

Into something I could mold

Press into me the most

Twisting and turning until it could be

The most like my true grit

Come home

Row your boat ashore
If you've been drifting

Get ever closer
To being yourself

It's time to come home
Take one step

Smile, laugh and play
Love unconditionally

Trust blindly
Never leave

Love wholly
In all that you are

Boundaries

It used to be

Others were always on top

I was not

To learn to bridge that gap

I had to push away

Turn others away

Place myself on top

Holding others near

So we can both be dear

Why me?

Why me

Why not me

I've had nights of cold

Days of cold

Moments of cold

Cold for days

Cold to last a lifetime

Yet I seek the light

My skin yearns for it

Scales grow thick from its lack

I thought nothing grew without light

My scales grew

How was that possible

My scales grew in search

Of what

Light peeks

They cease to grow

They shy away

They cringe

My scales cease

I am pleased

Why me

Why not me

Alone

Facing the start of the new day
Another twenty-four hours to fill
With nothing but solitude
Pushing back the covers
To look upon the emptiness
Within the compressing walls

I am not alone

Facing the streaming device
Another story to fill my time
With dialogue I can't contribute to
Familiar faces I have never met
Pushing back thoughts that won't be heard
By anyone but me

I am not alone

Facing birds perched on growing vines

Another sign of the familiar

With a promise that things will change

Pushing away my tears

To chance upon the changing tides

Within me the hope rises

I am not alone

Chrysalis

Magic unfolds in quiescence
Patching away the blight

Lumbering in the darkness
Echoing silent cries in the night

Handiwork of the truest self
To be embraced with might

Etchings of a phoenix
Tinges bleed into light

A rainbow trove in rising wings
I let myself light

Inner light

The light we hold

Within

Co-creates

With the universe

To make magic

Happen

Manifest

Our dreams

State of goodness

Health

Love

Relationships of all kinds

Empowering us to be

Ourselves

Free

Creative expression

It is who we are

Soul

Essence

Of all there is

I am deserving

I am deserving

Of sitting outside in peace

Of shopping for groceries without fear

Of not wanting to get out of bed

Of sleeping through the night

Of not going for a walk

Of not writing a poem a chapter a word

Of healing my burns

Of taking a nap at 5:17 pm

Of the two squares of chocolate I had after lunch

Of the rice and beans I had for lunch

Of the chocolate chip cookies I made for later

Of being embraced

Of being looked at in the eye

Of my twenty-minute yoga

Of wanting everything to go back as it was

Of folding myself into a cocoon

Of wrapping myself up in a blanket

Of being tired of wearing a mask

Of looking at my phone and finding a response

Of a full thirty-minute session, a minute no less

Of the tea tree to heal my acne

Of yet another show on Netflix

Of not wanting to stream anything ever again

Of reading a shitty novel

Of clean laundry and a dust-free house

Of liking what I see when I look in the mirror

Of being who I am

Woman

I
Am
A
Woman

Incredible

Beautiful

Happy

Empowered

Deserving

Worthy

Capable

Fertile

Lovable

Loving

Loved

Love

Generous

Kind

Compassionate

Friendly

Angry

Fearful

Worried

Anxious

Family

Working

Lazy

Worldly

Proud

Inspiring

Motivated

Dedicated

Responsible

Respectable

Faithful

Honorable

Crying

Small

Jealous

Earthly

Honest

Divine

Etheric

Universal

Valuable

I was on a path
Feeling unloved, unworthy, unseen
I am shedding it
Choosing me

I am honor, jewel, star
Feeling appreciated
No matter
I cherish me

I treat myself
Feeling loved, worthy, seen
Care for myself
Polishing me

I sparkle, twinkle, shine
Feeling loved
I am precious
I value me

Rebellion

Slaps me in the face
Senseless

A lifelong friend called
Me boring

Cracking a joke no one laughs
But me

Speak with another who doesn't ask
About me

Echoes of cackling fill

Emptiness

Perhaps my voice and choices

Don't matter

Opportunities knock

I answer

Hardships are a chance

To pivot

It creates a whirlwind

Disruption

The universe prodding me
To learn

I look in the mirror to face
My reality

My will changes my life
I matter

Realizing someone is always
Listening

Light sparks within
Guides me

My life path unfolds
I value

What matters most
Is love

Fourth, Anahata, heart

Give love, receive love, self-love, connect,
compassion, service, altruism

Surrounded by love

From within me
I whisper, my love
To me

From without me
I smile, coy
Looking in the mirror

From above me
Wearing, an outfit
The suits me

From below me
Walking, secure
In my own shoes

Journey to self-love

Through every bump, burn, and scratch

Wrinkle and pimple

Stretching near and far

I have been with you

In every curl, whisk, and fizz

Blip and dimple

Crowning me into oblivion

I have been with you

Every time I was left waiting

Withdrawn and taunted

Not wanting to be put down, let down

I have been with you

Through every trip and discovery

Connection and relation

A forced journey of awakening

I have been with you

Everything I have

For me and from me

The life I have lived

I have been with you

Every time I stand up

To be myself and who I am

All the love around me

I have been with you

I am love

Am I not?

I am all there is to love

And more

We all are

It's our essence

The heart of our being

Love is energy

And purpose

Belonging and meaning

Let love in

Love surrounds

Feel it

Recognize it

From within

And what others give

Everything

Is love

Including me

I forgive

For hiding

And being

Closed

Slow

And afraid

For inflicting

Not reaching

Calling

Texting

Or emailing

For dismissing

A need

Time

Space

And respect

For ignoring

Pushing away

Attention

Gifts

Or words

For giving

Away what

Was

Mine

My self

Compassion

I am compassionate

With myself

Forgive

Care

Prioritize

My needs above others

My being

Stand

Rise

Firm

Not risking myself

I don't seek

Attention

Sacrifice

Expectation

To be of service

Because I

Love

Honor

Value

In my power

Filled with

Love

Purpose

Conviction

I got here

In wholeness

Empathy

Kindness

Compassion

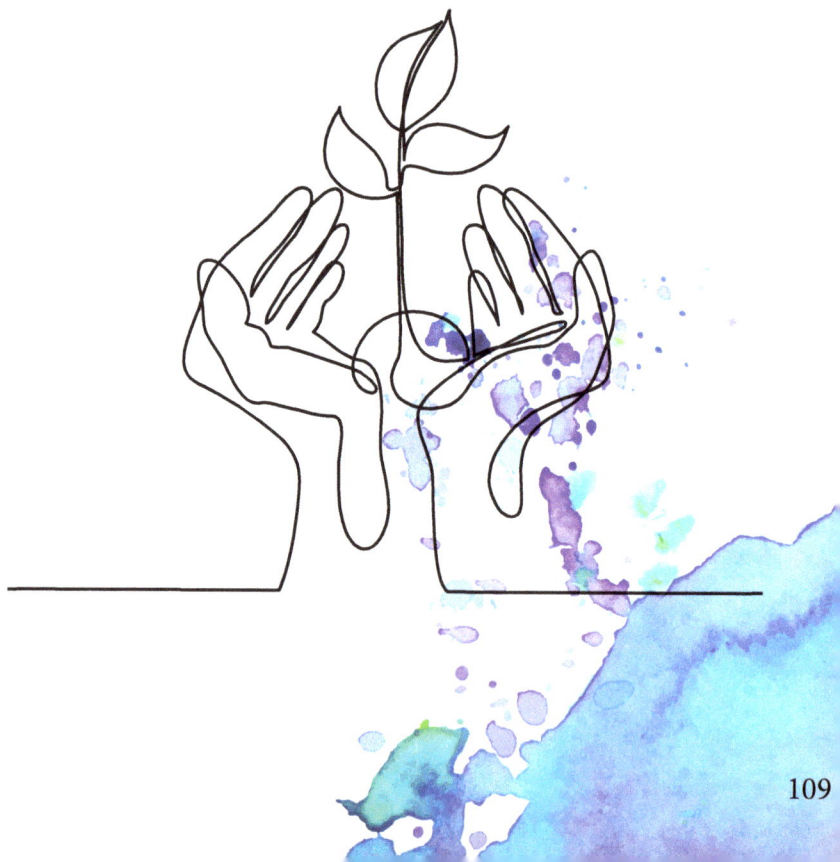

I am loved

The cardinal resting on my foot path
A curtsy before continuing on its way

The squirrel running across the empty street
Pausing for a car that will not come

The breeze that gently passes
Ruffling the leaves over the closed park

The dog that sniffs my legs
Before its owner nervously hurries it away

The stranger waving a silent greeting
As she crosses to the other side

The boat anchored in the harbor
Bankruptcy disabling its move

The lighthouse standing its ground
A symbol that wakens my heart

A friend with a rediscovered handicraft
The card waiting in the mail

A zoom that is scheduled
The new normal we've eased into

A solitary day spent in contemplation
When I realize I'm not alone

Many from near and far
Expressing what I already know

In the depth of my heart
I am never alone

I am loved
Deeply and by many

Loving

I love

Deep and hard

Connecting

Easing other souls with mine

I've been around a while

But there is one connection

Above all other

Monumental

It's been around for longer

How long I don't know

It's there

In every vision

In every dream

In every memory

In every experience

I carry it everywhere

Every conversation

Every book

Every screen

Every step

As if it were with me

Always

A witness

A partner

A confidant

The depth in the eyes

The smile lighting up a face

The veins tensing the neck

The lips pursing in discomfort

The longing in a being that is hard to fill

The sense of direction that guides

Knowing exactly what is wanted

The loss for what is gone

What is missing

Or hasn't yet arrived

The constant glances to the phone

The promptness of replies

The sense of responsibility

The loves

That comprise life

The twinkle in the eyes when they see me

A spirit relaxing in my presence

Silliness creeping in

As if we were still kids

Laughing at my jests

Noticing

Are they new shoes

Nice nail color

Gets me a refill

Without needing to check

A simple nod

A look in the eye

A crooked smile

A shake of the head

Silent ways of communicating

Fills my life by living

Gets me to tell the truth

Not even asking

I would love to see you

I would love you more

Soulsister

An easy companion
A silence that is home
Fills up our merry souls

Shared laughter rises up
Tears of joy cascading
Gripping our bellies

An eternal cord bonds
Who you are as you are
Who I am as I am

Exchanging gaping wounds
Hidden callouses
Through commiserate ears

Immutable roots rise

Cocooning in a web

Undying cherish

The universe conspires

As it always has

For our lives to make sense

You

Every decision I make has to do with you

Even when you weren't there

Even when I didn't know

And most certainly now that I know

There is no step in any direction

That is not with you in mind

I am drawn into your orbit

Because of that something bigger that binds us

The universe has been orchestrating

That you live your life as you have

And I live life as I have

And in its magic the two lives intertwine

Even now as I push away

It's not because I'm pulling away

I am coming into my own

So I am not defined by you

I live like me

Being who I am meant to be

Loving myself more

Not getting lost in you

Passing soulmates

How is it possible to love someone so much

When you barely know them

It's a flash of recognition

As if you've known them for all of time

There's a sense of trust and comfort

Knowing your deepest and darkest secrets

Are safely treasured in their hearts

They support and safeguard you

As you have done times before

In the past lives we don't recall

Except in the knowing look

We encountered mere moments ago

For whom

I moved here
For whom

For me
Because of whom

For my writing
Is of whom

For my social life
Revolves around whom

For my lifestyle
Colored by whom

For my solitude
Bare without whom

I moved here
Following a dream

A vision calling
Traversed the country

A quieter city
More relaxed

Opened up space
Changed my lifestyle

Healed my hurts
Felt more whole

More in love
Embodied me

I moved here
Searched

And found
Myself

Connection

Scenes flash
From previous
Lifetimes
We have been

Healer, villager
Friend, witch
Lawyer, worker
Lady of leisure

Through them all
Will always be
Our ability
To connect

We've done it

We'll do it again

Ourselves with nature

Animals and people

Some feel the connection

Within

Others

With themselves

A window

What could be

A portal

Into what is

Any level

Helps us sense

Their connection

Ours

Inner child

Youth and innocence

Cheeky smiles

Dipping fingers

Sweet cookie dough

Running out to play

It starts to rain

Matching in shades

Pale pink and lavender

Head to toe in butterflies

Unicorns dip into unruly hair

Dolls and stuffed koalas

Friends and playmates

Climbing on trees

Courageous limber ability

Connection with precious earth

Pretending to read a book

Immersed in short stories

Journeying to places

Never encountered

Needed remembering

New sights and things

Waiting lunchbox in hand

Yellow school bus

Riding in the back

A yellow tricycle

Pedaled around

A policeman that lay

Eating, sleeping, playing

Imagining, dreaming, creating

Living in make believe

Everything is possible

Magic happens

Every moment

Every day

I know

Feelings

Matter

Deserving

The way

I AM

Healed

Whole

Open

A channel

Fifth, Vishuddha, throat

Communicate, express, voice, creativity, truth, openness, purity

Unfolding

I need to know

Feel

My higher self says

It speaks to me

In my heart

Through my feelings

My chest expands

My mind explodes

Caterpillar turns to a butterfly

Two steps forward and one back

An eternal dance

A cycle that never ends

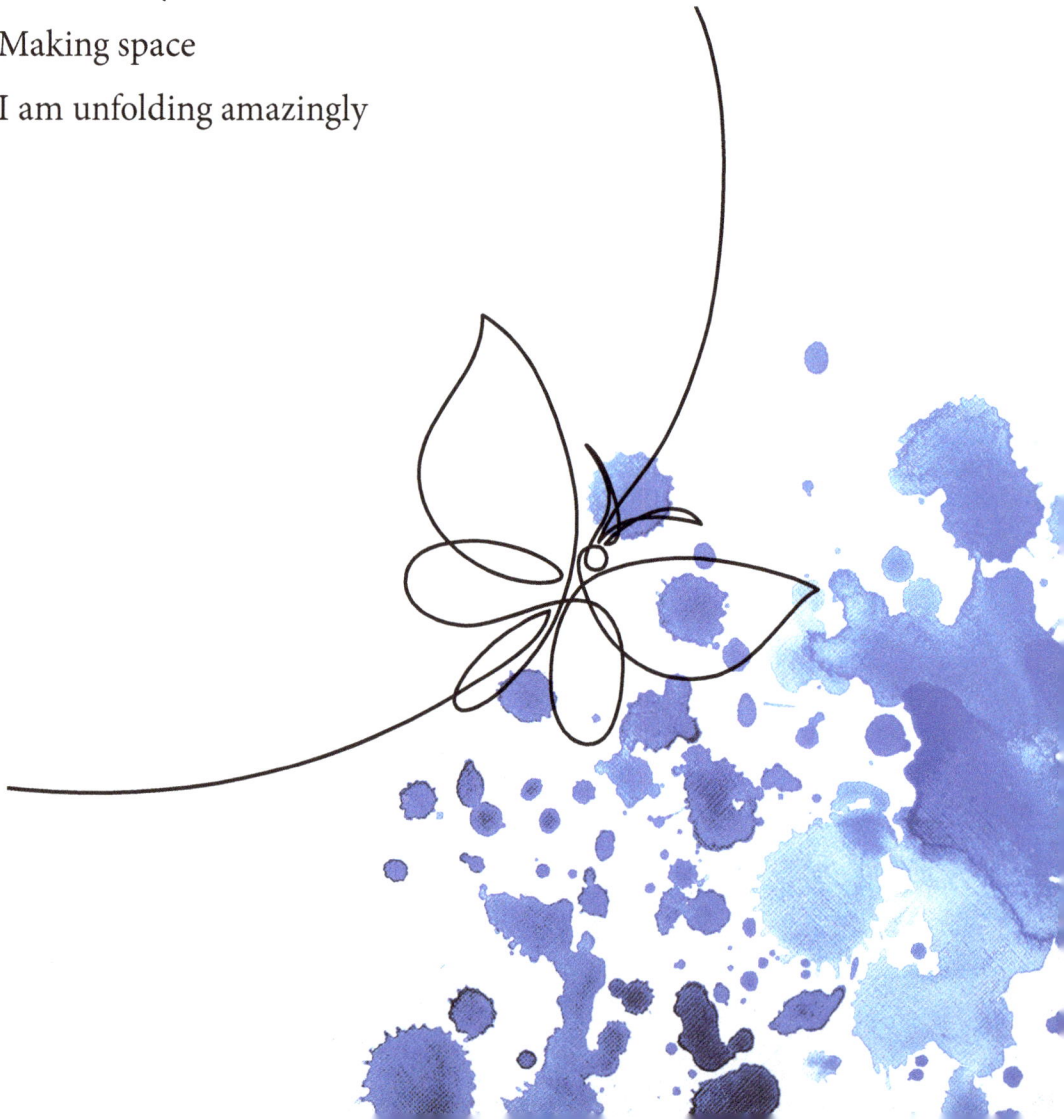

Not meant to be smooth and easy

Growth comes from breaking

A snake sheds its skin

Pieces of my skin fall

Making space

I am unfolding amazingly

My Voice

Be quiet he said and quiet I stayed

I didn't think my voice had value

I couldn't share had I wanted

My thoughts were a jumble

I didn't think my voice had value

To make sense of the mess

Of languages and cultures I compressed

I couldn't share had I wanted

I didn't know who I was

And where I belonged

My thoughts were a jumble

A tumble of sounds and silences

Moving so fast they made me stumble

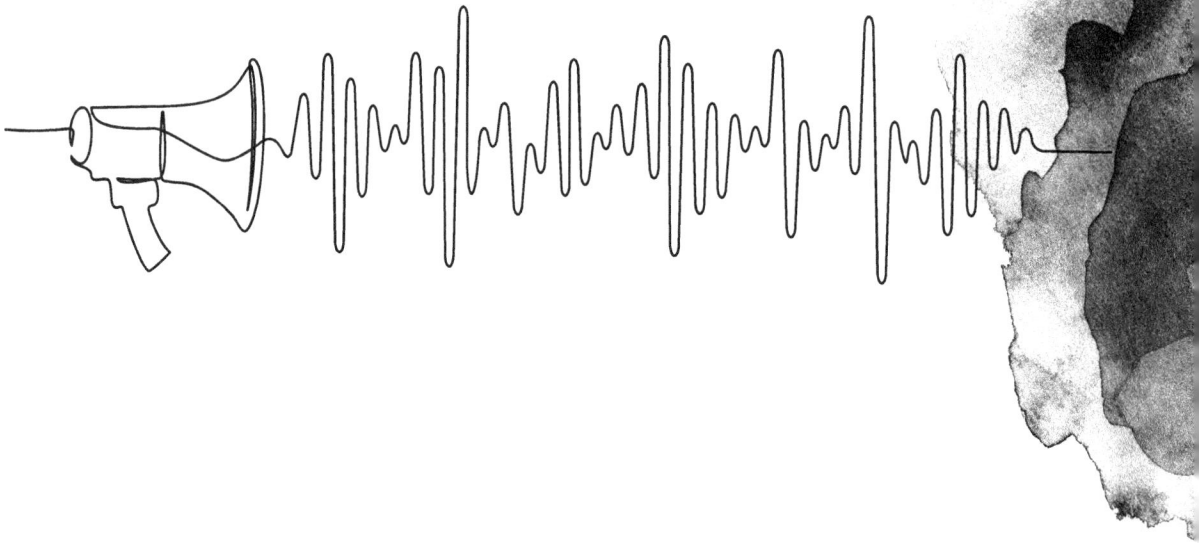

Speaking

I am worthy

I say it again

Repeat it

Like a mantra

A calling

The more I do

The more I believe

I hope

And pray

For my worth

Being loved

Calling attention

Receiving messages

Make sure I'm alright

Worthy connection

Friends and family

Needing and wanting

I am worthy

Of saying no

Protect myself

That is worth

Speaking my mind

Sharing my thoughts

Because they matter

My words

My life matters

Worthy to me

Others may disagree

That doesn't

Take away

I hold up

Regardless

Despite

I have value

I am worthy

My truth

I stay true
What makes me
Act accordingly
Behave and emulate

I express
Openly and clearly
What's in my heart
In my mind

Calmly and effortlessly
With conviction
And certainty
I share my truth

Authentic self

Oh Kali, exalted one

How you break me

Crack me open

I shed darkness

Density and weight

Break away the shackles

Feel freedom and ease

Walking in my own skin

Myself at home

In chaos and disruption

Pupa emerging

Shedding the cocoon

The old dies

The new rises

More me than before

Beautiful and magnificent

Rising from the fray

A quilt of patches

Oh Kali, thank you

For showing me how

To be my authentic self

I am

I am
Enough
Lovable
Beautiful
Accompanied
Always

I am
Healing
Empowering
Loving
Blissful
Magical

I am

Express

Speak

Voice

Listen

Myself

Words

Words pour
Like a cascade
Uninhibited unabashed
Flowing

Sometimes turbulent
Sometimes still
Always there
Ever present

They find me
Shake me
Prod me
And wake me

I allow myself
To move
So I can
Move others

Fusion Voice

I didn't think

Agua de panela with ginger and turmeric

My voice

Popcorn dipped in mango achar

Had value

Why would it

Chimi chutney on pakoras

I could not

Arepas with Tao Kae Noi and guacamole

Unscramble

For it to

Paratha filled with parmesan

Matter so

Tortillas rolled over dal sag

I grew quiet

Learning

From my readings
Books, articles, and greetings
Imprecise language
An oracle deck

From mistakes
Improvements and pitfalls
Telling not showing
Continuous edits

From what I do
Don't do
What I allow
Hold back

From criticism
Constructive to push
Become better
Extract the ore

From storytelling
Skill to acquire
Describe the world
Share it

From emerging emotions
Needing someplace to go
Healing acknowledged
Displayed in my being

From loss and gain
Watch it unfold
Hear them now
Call the tears

From judging eyes
Jiggly in a bikini
Hold the drinks
Watch others dance

From expectations
A woman is meant to
Want less
Say less

From letting go
Who I tried to be
Embracing instead
My own being

From what I wanted
I didn't know how
I still don't know
Yet I do it

From clinging
The part of my day
Connects me
To myself

From the distance

Behind screens

Barriers of safety

Giving me space to grow

From myself

I learn from the rest

The worst

The best

From people

Calls, messages, conversations

All who show me

Extending kindness

From love

I learn most

It's unconditional roots

The source of it all

The first fifty

It is a good sign

When an agent

Asks for

The first 50 pages

They are able

To discern

In those 50 pages

The novel's potential

Until I get through

The first 50 pages

I don't feel

I'm in the flow

I don't always reach the first 50

Have tried many things

Until I get to 49

Then I drop it

My challenge is that

To try something different

In the hopes

I will get past 50

I realized recently

The same applies to me

I need to get past 50

To feel in the flow

It could be as well

Until I'm past the first 50

I don't feel in the flow

Of my life

The first 50

May define many

But it doesn't

Define me

Reading

Read a lot and often

A book in an hour

If it's short

In thirty minutes

If it's poetry

In a week

If it's 1,000 pages

Non-fiction and novels

Spiritual and symbols

Poems and cooking

History and mystery

Mostly in English

Often in Spanish

Never in Hindi

Readers

When people read they feel alive

Words of inspiration

Poems, short stories, blogs, captions, novels

They see themselves

Live vicariously

Sing and dance

Laugh and cry with aching hearts

Fall in and out of love

Anger and sigh

See the world differently

Hopeful and faithful

Connecting dots they hadn't seen before

Between what is out there and what is in here

Nature, other realms, parallels, spirits

Remember we are part of something bigger

Connected, intertwined, one

Calls

Even the spam
Calls stopped
Change spared no one

For a time it was
Hard to speak
Think, sleep or dream

Too hard to comprehend
What we would do
What was to come

Was the resurgence

Of cacophonous calls

A sign of normalization

Or was it perhaps

A sign for us all

We can overcome

And rise

As do tides and days

Inevitably, indomitably

Beauty

A name means beautiful

It is not a coincidence

Nothing ever is

Becomes a life lesson

What is in a name

To express beauty

Embrace what's around

What is within

Identifying it internally

Opens the surroundings

The epitome of beauty
Neck that holds
A gorgeous smile
Lighting up the air
Igniting the aura

Tanned rose brown
Complexion of a being
Weak and saggy muscles
Knubbly and gnarly hands
All is beauty

Eyes that sparkle so brightly
Windows into truth
Illuminating the darkest
Innards of the soul
Come alive in beauty

Sixth, Ajna, third eye

Intuition, knowing, inner guidance, perception,

imagination, sight, inspiration

Expansion

I start with myself
No other point

Knowing myself
I grow

Seeing within
Is connecting with source

You are me
I am you

Together we reach
Expanding to others

The more I see
The more I love

Spreading throughout
We all expand

Manifest

Manifest

Dreams

Envision

Taste and smell

Fully sense

Feel

Integrate

Magic

Turn into present

Happens now

Reach

Here

Right

Fall into place

Come true

Flow

I am in flow
My cards alert me
The oracle has spoken
I run smoothly

Except for that
Quick course correction
A slight nudge
Steering the wheel

No more turns
Or detours needed
I've set my direction
Everything towards it

The road straight ahead
Visible to the eye
No traffic coming or going
Gentle and smooth

Spirit within
A drop in the universe
Sun Moon Fire
Water Air Earth

Events fall into place
A line of dominoes
Harmonious tumbling
Create preserve destroy

It's 3:33 am
I am guided and protected
Links of ancestors
Maiden mother crone

11:11 or
One two three four
I am on the path
Desire align manifest

My essence

I was born in the dead of the night

On the first Thursday of the year

The evening's curry pulsing through my veins

A full moon hung in the sky

Filling me in its aura

From then on and forever more

Appearing every 29 to 30 days

Reminding me of where I came

Setting free the trillion fireflies I hold within

Illuminating my essence

Ourselves

No excuses
No holding back
Full expression

Thoughts
Dreams
Desires

Visions
Moods
Emotions

All of it
All of me
All of you

In our glory

So we may

Bask

What makes you

You

And me, me

Unapologetically

Unabashedly

Ourselves

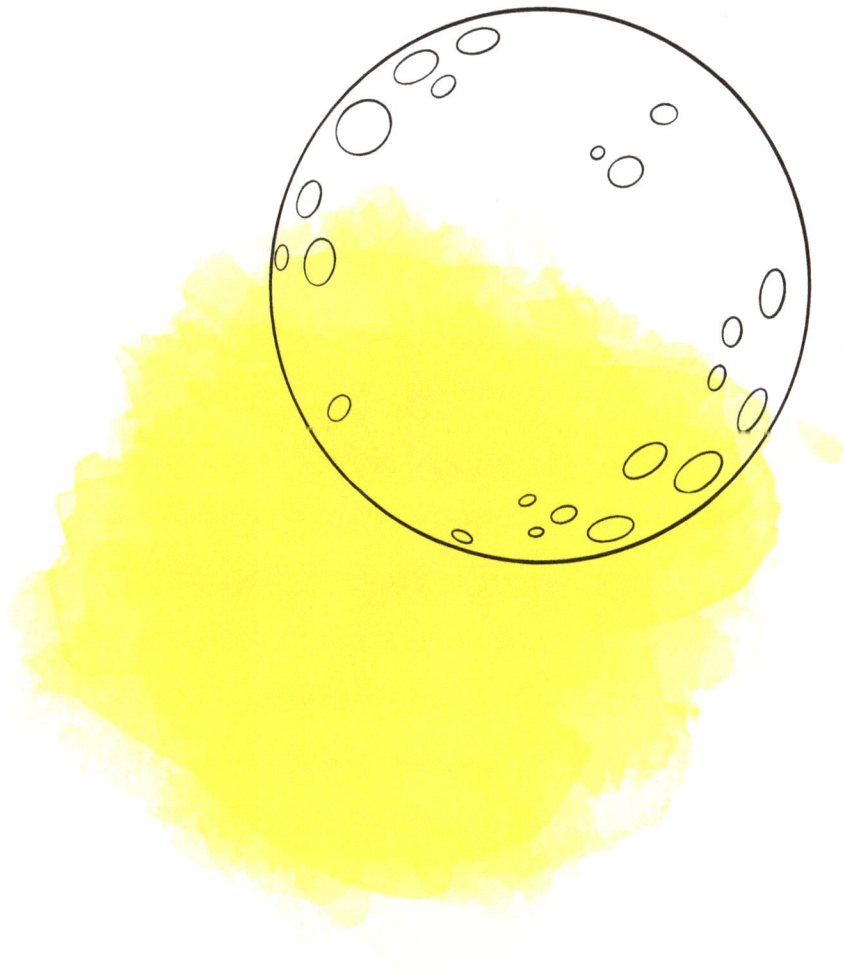

Full moon

The moon radiates
In its fullness
And even in its crescents

I was born under one
I just found out
Marking me

It's not a wonder
It speaks to me
In peaceful messages

Cradles me
Like a mother to its child
Soft and gentle

Nurtures my thoughts
What is possible
Discarding what is not

Moon magic

I love the moon
She is part of me
Moon magic

Surrender to your energies
Cutting away fears
Create new bonds

Tether me
To my chosen path
A life of purpose

Trusting in the unknown
I set myself free
Cords have been cut

They have a strong pull

Lean on me again

Says the moon

Again and again

I am always with you

Waxing and waning

The most loving thing

Do not act out of fear

Act out of love

Anxiety

I have not felt anxiety
Like I did
Today

My chest struggles
Up & down, up & down, up & down
This is more than breathing

Quick, quick, quick
Rises and falls
I gasp for air

I look up to make space
Open, open, open
Breathe

Palpitations
Pounding in my ears
I gasp for survival

I don't think I'll make it
I am all alone
I will always be

Accept your circumstances
They say
It is better to let go

I gasp for inclusion
What did I miss
I've tried and tried

I gasp for certainty
Mine went out for a ride
Never came back

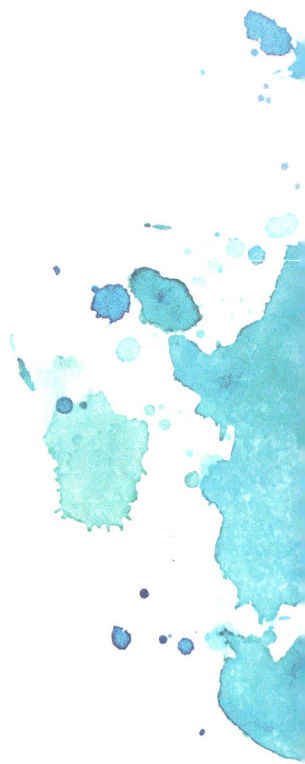

I gasp for myself
Somehow I'm still here
I pull myself up

One step
In front of the other
And the next…and next

I grab and grasp
Something I read
I surprise myself

I had it all along
Something to look forward to
Breathing settles

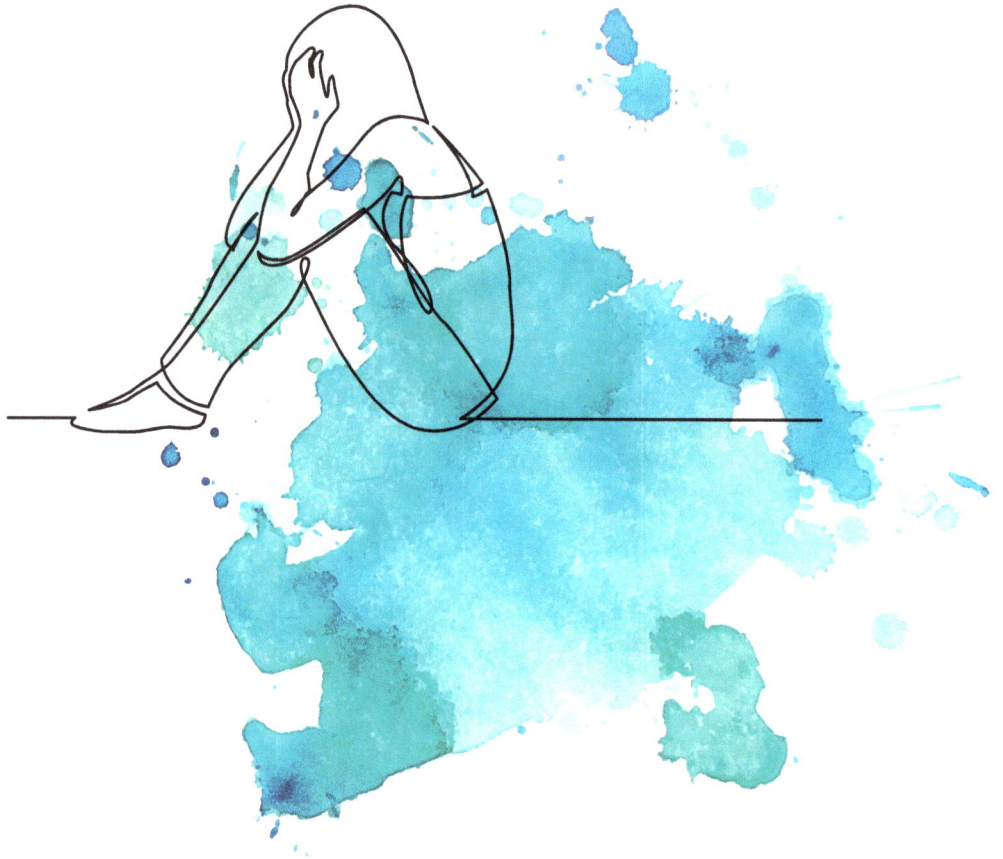

Five things

There are five things
Action we need
To be who we are

One is to summon our parts
Collect all the pieces
To put them back together

Two is to step into power
Not caring for judgment
To exercise our will

Three is to light the inner flame
Trust in ourselves
To listen to the guiding voice

Four is to express what we have

Authentic in our truth

To open to others

Fifth is to embrace life

All that it takes and provides

To love what it makes us

Living fearlessly and in trust

Loved in strong confidence

To be who we are

Growth

Isolation is loud
Silence speaks discomfort

Stillness itches
Shells are red and painful

Thighs collect
Rejection, judgement, resentment

Comfort tires with dust
Adjustment is achy and daunting

Unspoken words
Strangle digestion

Embracing grew in arms
Changing circumstances part of the journey

Pain yearns to be seen
It is better to be at peace

Have the will to choose
Not caring to be prodded and pushed

Shortcomings are part of the package
Despite the apparent lack

Learning from mistakes
Let the past go

It is never too late
Live the desired life

Embrace what is
It just is

Improve with specifics
Details are key to tell

Accept we are different
At home within ourselves

Being an odd ball
It is a beauty and an ache

Living is part of growth
Growth is part of living

Whole and complete

I am whole and complete

Even when I don't feel it

Even when something is missing

The parts of me that left with those

Who broke my heart

Hurt me or failed me

But these are all illusions

A heart cannot break

It's impossible

People left but others came

Nothing in me is missing

Hurts heal

People haven't failed

They lived their lives

I lived mine

They just happen to not coincide

I am still here

Whole and complete

Spark

Balanced and relaxed connection

Create and design oracles

Express calm feeling

Bake croissants from scratch

Exercise creativity in hobbies

Play a wooden flute

Explore interests in joy

Magical renditions through the lens

Discover the unknown

Gazing at stars in Atacama

Step strong into happiness

Read all the books I own

Natural in goodness

Donating what's not in use

Embrace what life is

One word at a time

Inner power lights fire within

Sparked from the universe

Throat

Words strangled
Silence reigned

Knotted terms
No comment

Thyroid diminished
Asthma surged

Muted gasp
Thought escaped

Opinions expressed
Notice made

Throat opened
Heart sang

Inner guidance

Nothing is more true

Than what comes from deep within

It's the truest expression

Of who I AM

Of source

Of my and our oneness

It's the voice

Of 1,000,000,000,000 voices

A cumulative act of all

The souls out there

That come to me

In my own special way

To reveal truths

That have been set forth

By the wisest

Of the wise

Truths that are truer

Than truth itself

I must heed this guidance

For doing anything but

Is denying myself

Denying the truth

Of who I AM

And so I must

I do

I choose to

Follow my inner guidance

Seventh, Sahasrara, crown

Spiritual connection, higher consciousness, wisdom,

divine, faith, presence, bliss

Goddesses

All their energies manifest
Shifting through moments

Kali's lightning strikes
What doesn't serve

Muse of creativity
Rising as Saraswati from the ashes

To embody Durga's power
Strident in her quest

Irradiating the abundant flow
Of Lakshmi's exquisiteness

Radha churning with love
For the divine

Shifting through asanas

In the yogini stance of Parvati

Sita's undying devotion

Of commitment to her family

Body, soul, and spirit intertwined

Through Lalita's sacred union

That brings about transformation

Maiden, Mother, and Dhumavati Crone

Inner energies wrapped

In total surrender of Chinnamasta

Holding Bhuvaneshwari's space

For all there is and everything in between

Shifting through moments

All their energies manifest

Inspired by Awakening Shakti: The Transformative
Power of the Goddesses of Yoga by Sally Kempton

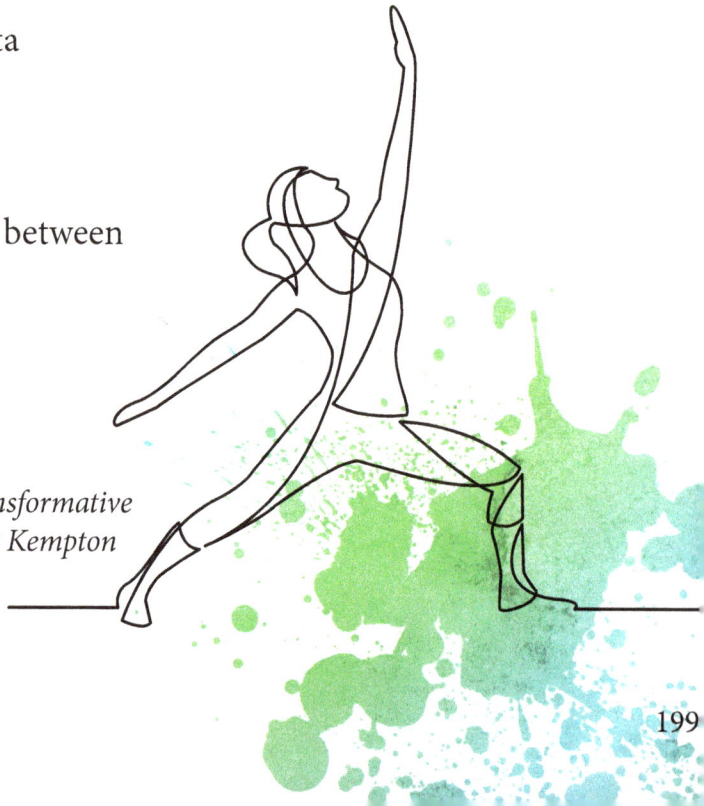

Divine feminine

Nurturing physical change

Unforeseen opportunities appear

Neurons finds new synapses

A convergence of co-creation

Surprise talents awaken

Making choices that ripple

Awakening to magic

Listening to the quiet mysticism

We all hold within

Invoke Kali

Destroy what is old and rusted
Clear the dust in the being
Soul, Mind, Spirit, Body

Banish and send it to oblivion
Suck out and cast away the gunk
Damp, Dark, Old, Meek

Burn my whole being
Letting in the new
Sparkly, Shiny, Squeaky, Clean

Harness the warrior spirit
Unleashing the light at the core
Power, Heart, Blood, Gut

Shine so bright it blinds
Dance fiercely conquering demons
Fear, Doubt, Hesitation, Uncertainty

Bring in transformation
Usher in love
Myself, Whole, United, One

Shiv Shakti

Shakti
In all there is
Feminine manifestation

Shiv
In universal consciousness
Masculine manifestation

Two
United into one
One sprung from the other

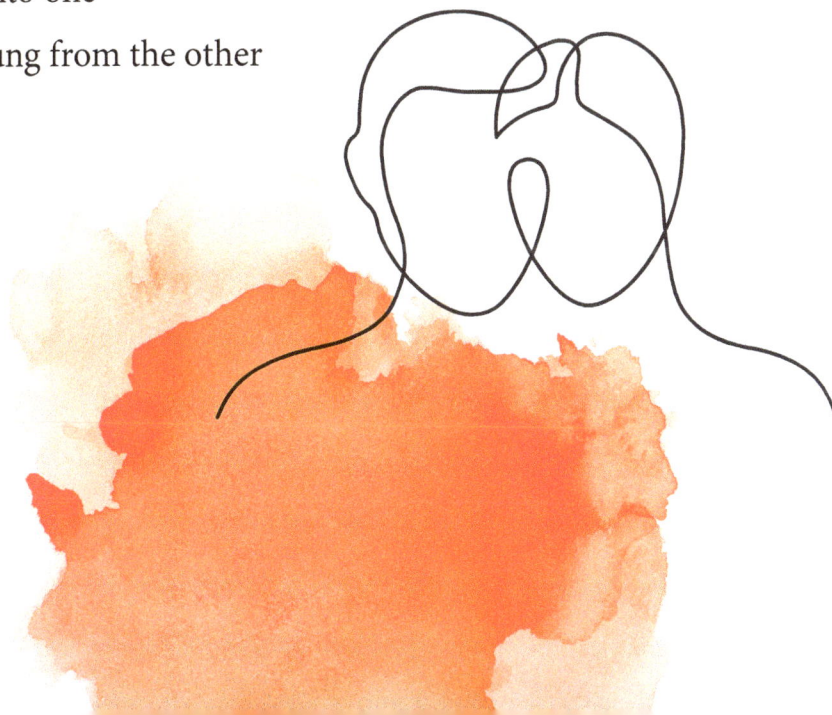

To embody fierceness
Inner warrior
Nurturing healer

To be reborn
We must die
Rise from the ashes

The way of the world
Endless cycle
Ebb and flow

The fire within
From death
Power rises

The love we hold
All there is
All that's needed

Connected

I call upon in gratitude

Unique as a flake of snow

Drawing out my strength

With all my wits

Reaching in my consciousness

Grounded in Mother Earth

Enlightened by Father Sky

Deep and loving

Everyone reaching out

Concern, care, and empathy

Connected with all there is

Part of the greatness

Of the universe

Faith

Faith waivers

Submerging in the waters of truth

What I see is real

Images etched in my mind

Ladden with details so sharp

I prick my finger when I reach out

The sea breeze fills my lungs

I taste the salt in the back of my throat

Touch the sea oats swaying

I wiggle my feet

Sand squishing between my toes

Leaving grit in my gums

I feel I am there
But it's only a dream
Tangible fades away

My faith waivers
A small fissure
Widening under pressure

A hand reaches out
I take it
The grip is firm and strong

Filled with so much love
I believe
What I touch is real

What I feel is true
What I see will come
Unwavering faith

Tiger

The tiger is my spirit animal

Have you many he asked

Of course, it is normal

We could all be helped

Harness the forces in our stead

Honoring and gracing

Prepared for what's ahead

Be better in the making

Dragons

A dragon is my spirit too

Not just one but two

Creatures that are mythical

Come to me when I ask them to

Or when they need me to

Believe in the magical

Full of guidance I need to

Pay attention and listen to

Make my life more practical

Union

It's a feeling I get
A sense of freedom
A wholeness that heals

My skin itches
Pores filled with ick
Roundness expands

A full eruption
Co-creative effort
Body intertwined with universe

Darkness is vanquished
Light descends
Immersing in aspects within

Courses throughout
Ever present
Unbreakable union

The vortex

Winds spinning
Chaos churns
Entropy reigns

Enter a void
Where nothing is
Emptiness

Call to be filled
Prayers
To the unknown

Grow comfortable
Not knowing
Surrender some more

Peace

May you
Have clarity
What you want

How you feel
Provides
Focus

May you
Have courage
Follow your purpose

Trust
What happens
Is your process

May you

Forgive

Who hurt you

And yourself

It's hardest

Yet necessary

May you

Feel peace

Today

You are

Where you

Need to be

Here

Air carries with it

Dense clouds ripe with rain

Ready to burst with the clap of thunder

Releasing upon us monsoon torrents

Wash away fears and doubts

Dirt of the sagging and old

Grime of the past

All we cannot change

Brings us to this present moment

Frogs creak and bees are abuzz

Birds chirp in the skies

Skins feel a waft of coolness

Relief from the intense summer heat

Coming to an end

Leaves hinting of color shading

A promise of cooler days ahead

In this moment all that matters

Shower from the heavens

Alerting us we are alive and well

This is our intention

To be here

Drop in the ocean

I am
A drop
In the ocean

As are
We all
One expanse

Together
We make
The larger

Individually
We carry
Ourselves

Uniquely
Yet intrinsically
Intertwined

All linked
Connected
ONE

I am that I am

I am my heart

My heart is open

Openness is giving

And receiving

Willingly and

Without judgement

I am myself

Without a care

Freely

Without restraint

I express

Who I am

I am my soul

Essence of my being

In this body

Another life

Another body

Same soul

I am a speck

Thread in a rug

Grain in a dune

Star in the cosmos

A part of all

I am that I am

I am that I am

Thank you to every single reader. It's for you that I write.

Thank you, Karen McDermott. I knew when serendipity made it so "easy" for me to join the retreat at Crom Castle, that this meeting wasn't by chance. Somehow, you would make an impact in my life, and you have done so in many ways. Thank you for giving me this opportunity. The moment you uttered, "Embody," I knew it was a winner.

Thank you, Jennifer Dinsdale for the delightful design of the cover.

Thank you, Ida Jansson for so beautifully capturing the essence of what I was expressing through your designs. The interiors are pure magic.

Thank you, Marcy Neuman for featuring me in your podcast. My voice was shaky as I read my poems out loud for the first time. It was an honor.

Thank you, Nailia Minnebaeva for providing me with the ingredients to do something with my social media feed and for the beautiful logo you created for me.

Thank you, Gretchen Hidell for motivating me to "push the button of bravery." The first poem I shared on social media gave energy to this whole process and you helped me feel courageous to do so.

Thank you, social media followers. I took a chance to share my poetry before I knew that it had a journey to embark on. Every single one of your likes, hearts, comments, and shares gave me the motivation to continue.

Thank you, everyone who gave input on the covers, namely Aleena Pitisant, Amy Kantorczyk, Bernadette Fava, Bilquis Ahmed, Daanish Khan, Dev Anand, Elif Egeli, Nasreen Khalid, Qais Sultan, and Stephanie Caunter.

Thank you, Mama, Papa, and Nieraj for encouraging me and for supporting my efforts to write poems. You are the rocks in my life.

About the Author

Sonee Singh is a cross-cultural seeker of deep knowing. She writes stories of self-discovery to encourage people to accept themselves for who they are and live life on their own terms. Her tales are of her character's definitive moments on their life's journey. The mystical and spiritual are integral in her storytelling, as is her multi-cultural background.

Sonee is of Indian descent, born in Mexico, raised in Colombia, and resides in the United States. When not traveling, reading, or writing, she indulges in meditation, yoga, and aromatherapy.

She holds a Bachelor of Arts in Biology and Society and a Master of Management in Hospitality from Cornell University, and a Master of Science in Complementary Alternative Medicine from American College of Healthcare Sciences. She is currently pursuing a Doctor of Divinity from the University of Metaphysical Sciences.

She worked in hospitality before practicing as a wellness coach. She is certified as an Integrative Nutrition Health Coach, International Certified Health Coach, Reiki Master, Registered Aromatherapist™, Certified Crystal Energy Guide, intuitive, and angel guide.

Her background and education often feature in her writing.

www.ingramcontent.com/pod-product-compliance
Lightning Source LLC
Chambersburg PA
CBHW060756150426
42811CB00058B/1423